BLS WORKING PAPERS

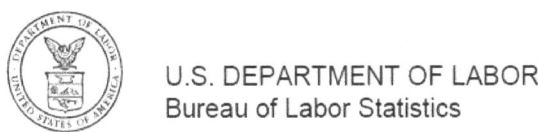

U.S. DEPARTMENT OF LABOR
Bureau of Labor Statistics

OFFICE OF PRICES AND LIVING
CONDITIONS

The Effect of Transfer Programs on Personal Bankruptcy

Jonathan D. Fisher, U.S. Bureau of Labor Statistics

Working Paper 346
October 2001

This paper is drawn from my Ph.D. dissertation at the University of Kentucky. I thank my chairman, William Hoyt, who has provide tremendous help throughout. This paper has also benefited from comments and suggestions from my committee: Mark Berger, John Garen, David Wildasin and J. Karl Scholz. Finally this paper has benefited from comments from participants at the SEA meetings and members of the University of Kentucky Microeconomics Workshop. The views expressed are those of the author and do not reflect the policies of the BLS or the views of other BLS staff members.

The Effect of Transfer Programs on Personal Bankruptcy

Jonathan D. Fisher*
Bureau of Labor Statistics
2 Massachusetts Ave., NE, Room 3105
Washington, DC 20212-0001
Telephone: 202-691-6596
Fax: 202-691-6583
Fisher_J@BLS.gov

*This paper is drawn from my Ph.D. dissertation at the University of Kentucky. I thank my chairman, William Hoyt, who has provided tremendous help throughout. This paper has also benefited from comments and suggestions from my committee: Mark Berger, John Garen, David Wildasin, and J. Karl Scholz. Finally, this paper has benefited from comments from participants at the SEA meetings and members of the University of Kentucky Microeconomics Workshop.

The Effect of Transfer Programs on Personal Bankruptcy

Abstract

Personal bankruptcy, Unemployment Insurance (UI), and Aid to Families with Dependent Children (AFDC) provide income- and wealth insurance. Since they have similar purposes, it should not be surprising that some households may use more than one of these programs in a year or that the programs are substitutes. This paper adds to the personal bankruptcy literature by examining this interaction between personal bankruptcy and transfer programs. First, the paper develops a new theoretical model of the decision to file for bankruptcy that shows the interaction between bankruptcy and the transfer programs. In this model, an increase in the transfer benefits decreases the probability the household files for bankruptcy. Next, the paper uses two different data sets to determine whether there is evidence of this interaction. Results suggest that decreases in either the average weekly UI benefits or average monthly AFDC benefits increase the number of bankruptcy filings.

I. INTRODUCTION

In 2000, over 1.2 million households filed for personal bankruptcy, which represents more than 1 percent of all U.S. households. Figure 1A shows that there has been a significant increase in the number of bankruptcy filings over the last twenty-eight years. Filings increased steadily since 1985, with the total number of filings exceeding one million per year since 1997. Interestingly, as inclusion of the GDP growth rate in Figure 1A suggests, bankruptcy filings do not seem to be sensitive to the business cycle.

Until recently, personal bankruptcy has not been researched intensively by economists.[1] There may be several reasons for this. First, compared to other government programs, a low percentage of households file for bankruptcy each year. Figure 1B shows that the number of Unemployment Insurance (UI) and Aid to Families with Dependent Children (AFDC) recipients exceeds the number of bankruptcy filers by at least a factor of five.[2]

Second, a perceived difference in the costs to society may lead to the disparity in research.[3] UI and AFDC entail federal and state outlays. In addition, economists studying these two programs focus on the negative work incentives of each program. Increases in the average UI benefits and average AFDC benefits have been found to decrease the probability the recipient works.[4] The costs of bankruptcy may be less transparent. Although the federal government incurs court costs for each bankruptcy filing, filers must pay a $175 fee, which internalizes at least a portion of the bankruptcy costs. The other direct costs of bankruptcy affect creditors, not consumers/taxpayers. However, creditors transfer these costs to individuals through a decrease in the supply of credit and/or an increase in the interest rate.[5]

While the costs of UI and AFDC may be more evident, the costs of bankruptcy are increasing as the number of filings increase. Concurrently, personal bankruptcy has attracted additional attention. However, there has been no research on the interaction between personal bankruptcy and government transfer programs. The main hypothesis proposed here is that changes in the government provided transfer programs affect the personal bankruptcy decision.[6] The paper derives a theoretical model that finds that personal bankruptcy and transfer programs are substitutes. Further, the paper finds empirical evidence that decreases in the average UI and AFDC benefits increase the number of bankruptcy filers.

2

The interaction between different government programs has been documented elsewhere. For example, the changes in the Earned Income Tax Credit (EITC) "explain 15.8 percent of the decline in welfare [AFDC/TANF] use over this time period [1993-1999]" (Grogger 2001, 28). Previous research had ignored the effect of the EITC on AFDC, but Grogger (2001) shows that doing so ignores a very important interaction between two government programs.

Analogous to EITC and AFDC, one cannot consider bankruptcy and the transfer programs in isolation since they have similar goals and have overlapping beneficiaries. In the Panel Study of Income Dynamics (PSID), 37.7 percent of the bankruptcy filers received income from at least one transfer program in the year they filed for bankruptcy.[7] Studying this interaction becomes increasingly important when changes in the programs are being considered. For example, significant changes occurred in the AFDC program, and the Congress proposed significant changes to bankruptcy. In 2001, the Senate proposed changes to the personal bankruptcy laws that would decrease the potential benefits to filing for bankruptcy, which could affect the number of UI and AFDC recipients.[8] In addition, the Federal government made significant changes to AFDC in 1997. These changes were designed to decrease the number of welfare recipients, which my results suggest would increase the number of bankruptcy filings.

The paper is laid out as follows. The next section provides an overview of bankruptcy laws. The third and fourth sections present the theoretical model. In the fifth section, the empirical model and results are presented. I conclude with a summary, caveats, and possible extensions.

II. PERSONAL BANKRUPTCY LAWS

An individual filing for bankruptcy chooses between Chapter 7 and Chapter 13.[9] Chapter 7 is designed for households with little or no wage income and is analogous to a liquidation of the household's assets. Chapter 13 is designed for households with regular wage income and is analogous to a reorganization of the household's debts. Of the 1.3 million personal bankruptcy filings in 1998, 403,500 (29.2 percent) were filed under Chapter 13.

In Chapter 7, the debtor must forfeit all assets exceeding the exemption levels to the Bankruptcy Court. In return, the bankruptcy court discharges most unsecured debts.[10] Secured debts are discharged only if the debtor forfeits the collateral. A bankruptcy trustee sells the non-exempt assets and distributes the money on a pro rata basis to the creditors. While the Bankruptcy Court is a Federal court, each state sets its own exemption levels, which determine the exempt assets. Federal exemptions exist and some states allow a debtor filing for bankruptcy to choose either the Federal or the state's exemptions.

Currently, Federal government exemptions include a $15,000 homestead exemption, an $8,000 exemption for personal property, a $2,400 motor vehicle exemption, a $1,000 exemption for jewelry, and an $800 wildcard exemption. A married couple, filing jointly, can double these exemptions. Other minor exemptions exist for work-related implements, professional books, tools, and other items.

The exemptions allow the individual to keep any property with a value below the exemption amount. For example, a homeowner filing for bankruptcy under the Federal code would be able to exempt up to $15,000 of equity in his home. If the filer has less than $15,000 of equity in the home, he is not required to turn the home over to the bankruptcy court when filing.[11] If the filer has more than $15,000 in equity, he must turn over the home in a Chapter 7 filing.[12] If the individual turns his home over to the bankruptcy court, he receives a payment equal to the exempt equity, in this example $15,000.

Individuals can also attempt to avoid these exemptions by arbitraging assets between categories. If the Federal filer has only $10,000 in home equity, he can sell some non-exempt assets and pay down the mortgage up to the exemption limit. Legal limits exist on this behavior and a judge can dismiss a bankruptcy filing if he feels that the individual is abusing the process.

Among the states, the range of exemptions is large. Pennsylvania allows the lowest exemptions (in dollars), allowing only a $300 wildcard exemption. However, Pennsylvania, like thirteen other states and the District of Columbia, allows the filer to choose either the Federal or state exemptions. Thus, filers in Pennsylvania should always use the Federal exemptions. Kansas is at the other extreme and offers an unlimited homestead exemption along with a $20,000 motor vehicle exemption.

The other option when filing for bankruptcy is Chapter 13, which is designed for debtors with wage or salary income. Filers do not turn over any assets to the bankruptcy court but instead propose a repayment plan for a *portion* of the outstanding debts. Usually, the plan lasts three to five years. If the repayment plan is successfully completed, the filer receives a discharge of some of his unsecured debts.

III. AN OVERVIEW OF THE THEORETICAL MODEL

In this section, I develop a model of the individual's decision to file for bankruptcy. In the model, the tradeoff between current consumption and future consumption is central to the household's decisions. When filing for bankruptcy, the household may lose a significant number of assets, which are its source of future consumption in this model. However, the individual can increase current consumption when filing for bankruptcy. The model shows this tradeoff between current and future consumption and the decision to file for bankruptcy in a utility-maximizing framework. The presence of the transfer programs affects this tradeoff, and therefore the transfers affect the decision whether to file for bankruptcy. Previous research did not consider that the household might receive other transfers and that these transfers might affect the bankruptcy decision. Here, the individual can receive the transfer benefits instead of filing for bankruptcy, or the individual can receive the transfer benefits and file for bankruptcy.

Income shocks also affect the bankruptcy decision. Previous research assumed negative wealth shocks rather than income shocks lead to a filing.[13] In my model, an individual borrows in the first period not knowing period two income. If the individual has an income shock in the second period from a job loss or the loss of a family member through divorce or death, the individual may file for bankruptcy.[14]

The model assumes that the risk-averse individual lives three periods with each period corresponding to a different stage in the individual's life. In the first period, the individual begins working and borrows against future earnings. In the second period, the individual continues to work and has the decision whether to repay the loan. Finally, the individual retires in the third period and consumes the assets acquired in the first and second periods not already consumed.

The first period can be thought of as the early working career of the individual. For income, the individual receives wage income (K_1) and borrows (B). The individual agrees to repay the principal and interest in the second period but also retains the right to file for bankruptcy. The individual may use the borrowed money to increase consumption in the first period, but individual may also use it to purchase durable goods that will be consumed in the second and third periods.

In the second period, the individual again has wage and salary income, K_2, which comes from the known probability distribution function $f(K_2)$. Before the second period begins, the individual knows the distribution of wages but does not know the realization of his income until after the second period begins. In part, this uncertainty about second period income leads to the bankruptcy filing. If the individual knew period two income with certainty, he would be less likely to borrow beyond his ability to repay.[15] The individual also receives government-provided transfer benefits, $T(K_2)$, if eligible.

The individual has three decisions in the second period (1) whether to file for bankruptcy, (2) whether to sell any of his assets, and (3) whether to save additional income. First, the individual decides whether to file for bankruptcy. If the individual does not file, he repays the principal and interest, $B(1+r_B)$, where r_B represents the interest rate. If the individual files for bankruptcy, he repays some amount R ($<B(1+r_B)$), which depends on several factors: wage income (K_2), assets (P_1), the amount borrowed (B), and the bankruptcy exemptions (E_P).

The second decision is whether to sell some of the assets acquired in the first period. For example, an individual can withdraw money from an Individual Retirement Account before it matures, but the individual must pay a penalty for early withdrawal. Therefore, the individual faces transaction costs if he sells some of these assets in the second period. Another example is costs associated with selling a home, which includes realtor costs, closing costs, moving costs, and opportunity costs.

Thus, if the individual sells some of his assets in the second period, he incurs a proportional transaction cost, $1-\eta$ ($0 < \eta < 1$). If he sells an asset worth one dollar, he only receives $\$\eta$ for this asset. By assumption, the individual can costlessly sell a portion of his assets, θ ($0 <\theta< 1$).[16] If the individual decides to sell some of his assets, he may choose to sell only a portion of the assets. The proportion of assets he actually sells equals φ, where $0\leq \varphi \leq 1$. Thus, the individual can increase period two income and hence period two consumption by as much as $\theta + \eta(P_1 - \theta)$, if $\varphi=1$.[17]

The last decision in the second period is also related to the individual's assets. Rather than sell assets, the individual can choose to save additional assets. The individual may want to increase period three consumption by saving in the second period. The last decision is how much to save, S_2, where $0 \leq S_2 \leq K_2 + T(K_2) - B(1+r_B)$. These three decisions plus the individual's income and transfer benefits determine period two consumption and period three consumption.

In the third period, the individual retires. Consumption in the third period depends on the amount of assets saved in the first two periods and not consumed or lost to bankruptcy in the second period. Therefore, period three consumption depends entirely on the decisions made in the second period.

IV. THE PERIOD TWO AND PERIOD THREE TRADEOFF

The individual decides whether to file for bankruptcy in the second period after his period two income has been revealed and after he has made his first period decisions. The individual's decision whether to file depends, in part, on the tradeoff between consumption in period two and consumption in period three. When filing for bankruptcy, the individual repays less to his creditors, which increases period two consumption. However, the individual must turn over any assets above the exemption level to the bankruptcy court. Since these lost assets represent the individual's main source of period three consumption, a bankruptcy filing can greatly diminish consumption in the third period.

To best see this tradeoff, budget constraint (1) in Figure 2 shows the constraint between period two and period three consumption if the individual does not file for bankruptcy or the transfer program benefit. If the individual could costlessly transfer assets between the two periods, the budget constraint would have a constant slope equal to negative one, and both intercepts would equal $K_2 - B(1+r_B) + P_1$. However, the individual incurs a transaction cost $(1-\eta)$ on the sale of a portion of his assets in the second period. If the individual sells all of his assets in the second period, the maximum consumption equals $K_2 - B(1+r) + \eta*(P_1-\theta) + \theta$.

Next, I introduce bankruptcy into the model. If the individual files, he loses all non-exempt assets leaving assets worth E_P in the second period. Figure 2 shows three different bankruptcy budget constraints, constraints (2) through (4), each of which could occur depending on the magnitude of the benefit to filing.[18] The position of the new intercepts depends on the size of the benefit. As the benefit to filing increases, both intercepts increase. However, even if the individual benefits from filing, the y-intercept does not necessarily increase (see Appendix for this proof).[19]

With budget constraints (3) and (4), the individual always files for bankruptcy if he benefits from filing. Thus, the magnitude of the benefit to filing plays an important role in the decision to file for bankruptcy. Alternatively, an individual with constraint (2) may not file for bankruptcy, depending on his marginal rate of substitution. Someone with a smaller benefit may or may not file for bankruptcy. Of the three budget constraints in this figure, the most interesting case is the lowest budget constraint, line (2). The following focuses on the decision rule for someone with this smaller benefit.

The relevant budget constraint for the individual in this interesting case is now a portion of the bankruptcy constraint and a portion of the no-bankruptcy constraint. From the y-intercept to the point where the two budget constraints intersect, the relevant portion of this new budget constraint comes from the no-bankruptcy budget constraint. From the point of intersection to the x-intercept, the relevant portion comes from the bankruptcy constraint. The solid-line budget constraint in Figure 3 shows this.

Next, I include the transfer benefits. In the second period, if an individual is eligible to receive transfer benefits, then the x- and y-intercepts both increase by size of the transfer benefits, $T(K_2)$. The decision of some individuals about whether to file for bankruptcy is not affected by the introduction of the transfer benefits. If the individual does not file for bankruptcy before the introduction of the transfer benefits, he will not file after their introduction. Similarly, an individual who values period two consumption highly or has a large benefit to filing for bankruptcy will be unaffected by the introduction of the transfers. This means that the individuals with budget constraints (3) or (4) from Figure 2 are not affected by the introduction of the transfer benefits.

Someone who has a small benefit to filing may file for bankruptcy without the transfers but not file after their introduction. In Figure 3, the solid-line budget constraint represents the budget constraint for the interesting case derived from Figure 2. In a world with no transfer benefits, an individual with indifference curve U_0 maximizes utility by filing for bankruptcy. When the transfer benefits are introduced, the decision to file for bankruptcy is altered in Figure 3. Since indifference curve U_0 intersects but is not tangent to this new budget constraint, the individual does not file for bankruptcy when the transfers are introduced. Thus, the introduction of the transfer programs decreases the probability the individual files for bankruptcy.[20]

Finally, Figure 4 shows how an increase in the transfer benefit decreases the probability the individual files for bankruptcy. With the smaller benefit, the individual maximizes utility by filing for bankruptcy, represented by indifference curve U_0. When the individual receives the larger benefit, the budget constraint shifts out by $\Delta T(K_2)$. With the new budget constraint, the individual maximizes utility by receiving the transfer benefit and not filing for bankruptcy, represented by indifference curve U_1. Thus, an increase in the transfer benefit decreases the probability an individual files for bankruptcy.

By receiving the transfer benefits, the household increases utility by retaining its assets that would be lost in bankruptcy. Although the household repays more to its creditors when it does not file, the gain in future consumption more than offsets the loss in current consumption for this household. Gruber (1999) provides supporting evidence that some UI filers could be in such a situation. Gruber finds that many households have enough assets to supplement any UI benefits they receive in order to smooth consumption. These types of households that have assets and are eligible for UI are the types of households that may receive the UI benefits rather than file for bankruptcy since they have assets that may be lost in bankruptcy. However, Gruber also finds that approximately one-third of workers cannot replace even 10 percent of their lost income from wealth holdings (p 3). These households are the ones that are likely to file for bankruptcy and receive the UI benefits, if they become unemployed.

V. EMPIRICAL MODEL AND RESULTS

The following presents the empirical results using two different data sets, both covering the years 1989-1996. First, I use data aggregated to the state. Then, I use a household-level data set, the Panel Study of Income Dynamics (PSID). From the theoretical model, the decision to file for bankruptcy depends on several factors including the benefit to filing, the income, the transfer benefits, and the individual's marginal rate of substitution. The following describes the variables used in the household-level specifications and their state-level equivalents.

First, to control for the benefit to filing, I construct a financial benefit to filing variable from the PSID, which is the traditional measure used in the literature.[21] Mathematically, the variable equals:

$$Benefit_{it} = Max\{Debt_{it} - Max[(Wealth_{it} - exemptions_{it}), 0], 0\}. \tag{1}$$

Debt represents the unsecured debts of household i in year t. Wealth equals the household's wealth. The exemptions are the relevant state bankruptcy exemptions for the household, which vary not only by the state of residence and year but also by the different characteristics of the household.[22] For example, married filers who file jointly can double the exemptions in some states. Thus, the exemptions are doubled for married households if the state allows it. Similarly, only homeowners can claim the homestead exemption. For households that rent, the homestead exemption equals zero. In states that allow an unlimited exemption, the homestead exemption is set equal to the value of the home, as reported by the household. Therefore, the exemptions used in equation (1) reflect the exemptions for the specific household, depending on these different characteristics of the household and the state laws.

The first term in equation (1) represents the debt forgiven since unsecured debts are forgiven. The second term represents the lost assets. If wealth is larger than the exemptions, then the household loses property when it files. If wealth is smaller than the exemptions then the household loses no property and this term equals zero. The benefit is therefore the debt forgiven minus any lost assets. In the specifications presented below, I also include the square of the financial benefit to allow for a non-linear effect. Table 1 compares the means for several variables used in the PSID specifications. For the filers, the average financial benefit equals $3,478 while it equals $1,377 for the non-filers.

In the state data, I use the state bankruptcy exemptions rather than the financial benefit to filing. I use three different measures of the bankruptcy exemptions in each specification presented. The first variable equals the dollar value of the homestead exemption, if the state does not have an unlimited homestead exemption. If the state's homestead exemption is unlimited, the state receives a zero for their homestead exemption. Instead of arbitrarily top-coding the unlimited homestead exemption, I create another variable that equals one if the state has an unlimited homestead exemption and zero otherwise. This dummy variable captures the effect of the unlimited exemption, and the exemption variable denominated in dollars captures the effect of the homestead exemption in states without the unlimited exemption. The third variable equals the sum of the dollar value exemptions for personal property, automobiles, tools of the trade, jewelry, and any wildcard exemption.

As a further measure of the state's laws, one additional variable is included. Some states allow creditors to garnish the wages of delinquent debtors. If a debtor files for bankruptcy, wages cease being garnished. Thus, a state that allows the garnishment of wages is predicted to have a higher bankruptcy filing rate. The garnishment variable equals one if the state permits garnishment.

Another important determinant of the decision to file is the household income. A debate about income has been on going in the bankruptcy literature. White (1991) and Fay, Hurst, and White (2001) argue that income should not be related to the filing rate since individuals behave strategically when filing for bankruptcy. According to their theory, a person files as long as there is a financial benefit from filing, regardless of income. Alternatively, Sullivan, Warren, and Westbrook (1989) argue that individuals file for bankruptcy when a negative event occurs, such as a loss of a job or a divorce. They argue that a decrease in income leads to a bankruptcy filing rather than any strategic behavior by the individual.

In the theoretical model developed above, it is both income and the size of the financial benefit that affect the filing rate. A negative income shock may make it more difficult for the individual to repay the loan in full, which contributes to the decision to file for bankruptcy. However, the individual also must have a positive financial benefit from filing. This represents a mixture of the two competing theories, although it is closer to Fay, Hurst, and White. Thus, total family income is included as well as a dummy variable indicating whether family income decreased between t-1 and t.[23] For the filers, average household income equals $23,270, while income for the non-filers equals $31,259 (Table 1).

In the state-level regressions, I include the per capita income of the state. To control for shocks to income, the unemployment rate and the percent divorced in the state are included as well.

The next important determinant from the theoretical model is the transfer benefits. Since states determine the bankruptcy exemptions, the paper focuses on three transfer programs also administered by the states. As measures of the transfer benefits, the paper uses the average weekly UI benefits, the average monthly AFDC benefits, and the average Medicaid benefits per capita.[24] Both sets of results use these three variables. While the PSID survey does include actual UI and AFDC benefits received and whether the household received Medicaid, I use the average state benefits instead. Since the household can choose whether to receive the benefits if it is eligible, the model would include a choice variable for the household if I used the actual benefits received rather than the state averages.[25]

While the specifications do not use the actual benefits received in any reported specifications, using the PSID data to compare the filers and non-filers provides useful information. Eleven percent of those who did not file for bankruptcy in the PSID received UI, while 15.5 percent of the filers received UI in the year they filed (Table 1). At the 5 percent level of significance, I reject the hypothesis that the two proportions are equal. The percentage of filers that received AFDC is also slightly higher than the non-filers, but the proportions are not statistically different.[26]

The last determinant of the individual's decision whether to file for bankruptcy is the marginal rate of substitution (MRS). While this cannot be measured directly, several variables can proxy for it. First, I include a set of household characteristics. Two dummy variables indicate the level of education of the head of the household. The first is whether the head graduated college. The other equals one if the head's highest degree received is a high school diploma. Since college graduates are generally paid more than those without a bachelor's degree, they may need bankruptcy less. However, college graduates may have access to more credit and be more aware of the legal remedies in bankruptcy, which could make them more likely to file for bankruptcy.

If someone in the household owns a business, the family may be more likely to file for bankruptcy. Owners of unincorporated businesses are personally liable for the business debts, which may make them more likely to file if the business is in trouble. The age of the head is expected to have a non-linear effect on the probability of filing for bankruptcy. Younger households are just beginning to gain access to credit, and it may take some years to borrow enough for them to get into serious financial trouble. However, after a certain age, the household may have paid off its major debts such as the home and therefore it has a lower probability of filing for bankruptcy. To capture this effect, I include the age and age-squared of the head. Next, the family size is included. For a given income, a larger family may be more likely to file for bankruptcy since they have to spread income out over more individuals.

Also included as a proxy for the MRS are characteristics of the state since the propensity to file may differ across states. First, the number of individuals employed in the legal sector in the state divided by the total employment in the state is used. Next is the state bankruptcy filing rate in t-1, which captures the stigma associated with bankruptcy. Third, the state per capita income growth is included, which equals the change in per capita income between t-1 and t in the state. Finally, I include the standard deviation of per capita income over 1980-1996, which varies across states but not over time.

Similar variables are included in the state-level regressions as the ones discussed above from the PSID specifications. In addition, several variables are included in the state-level regressions that have no similar variable in the household results. To control for business cycle factors and other factors that might lead to bankruptcy filings, the percentage of employment in the nine broad categories of industry is used. The nine sectors are agriculture, mining, construction, manufacturing, wholesale, retail, service, transportation and utilities (TPU), and finance, insurance, and real estate (FIRE). To control for the credit market, the number of bank offices located in the state divided by the population of the state is included. Finally, year dummy variables are included. In part, the year dummies control for any changes in the attitudes of the country that do not vary across states but do vary across time.

With all of the variables defined, the specification is as follows:

$$Prob(Bankruptcy_{it} = 1) = \Phi(\beta_0 + \beta_1 X_{it} + \beta_2(benefit_{it}) + \beta_3(Y_{it}) + \beta_4(T_{it}) + \beta_4(Z_{it}) + u_{it} > 0); \quad (2)$$

where $Bankruptcy_{it}$ equals one if household i filed for bankruptcy in year t, X_{it} is the vector of household characteristics, $benefit_{it}$ equals the financial benefit to filing, Y_{it} equals the household income and the income shock variables, T_{it} are the potential transfer program benefits, Z_{it} is a vector of state characteristics, and u_{it} is a white noise error term. Assuming $\Phi(.)$ is the standard normal distribution, equation (2) can be estimated using a probit.[27]

In the state-level regressions, the dependent variable equals the state bankruptcy filing rate in year t, which equals the number of personal bankruptcy filings divided by the population.[28] Rather than using a linear probability (LP) model, the filing rate is transformed using a logistic transformation. If F_{it} is the filing rate of state i in year t, then the dependent variable equals $ln[F_{it}/(1-F_{it})]$. This transformation solves two problems introduced by the LP model. First, the LP model does not restrict the predicted proportion to lie between zero and one. In addition, it restricts the estimated effects to be linear. Using the logistic transformation corrects both problems.[29]

A. State-level results

Although the theoretical model uses households as the unit of interest, I begin by presenting the empirical results using the state-level data. Since 1 percent of U.S. households file for bankruptcy each year, it may be harder to find effects using the household data than with the state data. In fact, over the eight years of the PSID sample used, only 187 households filed. In contrast, there are 34,586 other observations with no filing.[30] By using aggregated data and using the proportion of households that file for bankruptcy each year, there is more variation in the dependent variable using the state data. The state data also provide an overview of the analysis and supporting evidence from a different data set.

Table 2 reports the results of the regressions using the state data. In the second column of Table 2, I add region fixed effects to the variables used in the first column.[31] By including state fixed effects, there is very little independent movement between the fixed effect and the unlimited exemption variable. Only Iowa increased its homestead exemption to unlimited while Minnesota was the only state to change to a limited exemption from unlimited during the period. Thus, I use region fixed effects.[32]

In both columns of Table 2, the transfer benefit coefficients are negative and statistically significant except for the Medicaid coefficient in column (2).[33] The two measures of the exemptions denominated in dollars are the wrong sign. States with higher exemptions should have a higher filing rate, but the coefficients are negative. However, the coefficient on the unlimited variable is positive and significant in both columns, as predicted. The other variable that controls for the laws of the state is the garnishment variable. Its coefficient is positive and significant in both columns, as predicted.

The per capita personal income variable is negative in both columns, but it is only statistically significant in column (1). The sign matches the findings of the theoretical model developed above. States with a lower per capita income have a higher filing rate. The two variables that represent negative income shocks both have the expected sign as well. The coefficient on the unemployment rate is positive in both columns and is statistically significant in column (2). The other variable is the percent divorced, which is statistically significant and positive in both columns.

Several signs do not match predictions. First, states with a higher percentage of people with health insurance have higher filing rates.[34] Next, the variable controlling for the number of lawyers, legal employment per capita, is negative and significant. It could be that fewer people file for bankruptcy after consulting with a lawyer. The other coefficient that does not match expectations is the population coefficient. However, both the population and the percent of the population that live in a Metropolitan Statistical Area (MSA) proxy for the stigma. And, the MSA coefficient is positive and significant, as predicted. The sign of the remaining coefficients in the state-level results match expectations.

B. PSID results

While the results using the state data provide support for the hypotheses, the theoretical model uses the household as the decision-making unit. Thus, the PSID is a more appropriate data set to study these questions. In 1996, the PSID asked the participating households a set of questions regarding all the household's bankruptcy filings.[35] All households were asked if anyone in the household had filed for bankruptcy and if so, in what year. The data used span the years 1989-1996, making 34,773 observations. Of the almost 35,000 observations, only 187 households filed for bankruptcy and had values for all of the other variables.[36]

Table 3 presents the results using the PSID.[37] The variables included in column (1) closely match the variables from Fay, Hurst, and White, and I add the transfer program variables.[38] In column (1) of Table 3, the transfer coefficients are the wrong sign. The remaining coefficients match the findings of

Fay, Hurst, and White except the reduction in income variable, but that coefficient matches expectation in my results and not in Fay, Hurst, and White.

The financial benefit variable matches expectations. In the state-level results, only the unlimited variable coefficient was statistically significant, while the exemptions denominated in dollars were statistically insignificant. In the PSID results, the financial benefit and benefit squared coefficients are statistically significant. Since I measure the variables more precisely in the household data, this result is not surprising. Further, the income coefficient is negative and significant as predicted. This finding matches the theoretical model developed above where income shocks rather than wealth shocks lead to a bankruptcy filing.

Column (2) of Table 3 uses the same variables but excludes the lag of the bankruptcy rate. In this specification, the signs on the two state income measures change sign, but both remain insignificant. Importantly, the UI coefficient becomes negative and statistically significant, while the AFDC and Medicaid coefficients remain positive and insignificant.

Finally, column (3) of Table 3 adds several other household characteristics. The results in this column match the results from column (2). The UI coefficient is negative and significant. As for the variables added, the coefficients match expectations. The first variable equals one if the head missed work during the year because he was sick or because someone else in the household was sick. This represents another potential income shock since the individual missed work. If the head missed work, the household is more likely to file for bankruptcy. An increase in the tenure of the head of the household decreases the probability the household files, indicating that longer job stability decreases the probability of a bankruptcy filing. The 'male is head' variable equals one if the head of the household is male, and the married variable equals one if the head is married. Both coefficients are statistically insignificant. Households headed by a divorced, widowed, or separated person are more likely to file for bankruptcy than households headed by a single person.

Thus, I find evidence using both data sets that UI and bankruptcy protection are substitutes. From the PSID results, I find that an 8 percent increase in the average UI benefits decreases bankruptcy filings by approximately 3.3 percent.[39]   I also find evidence that AFDC and bankruptcy protection are substitutes, but I only find evidence in the state data. A 4 percent increase in the average AFDC benefits decreases bankruptcy filings by 1.5 percent. However, I do not find evidence that Medicaid benefits affect the number of bankruptcy filings.

When looking at the eligible populations, the results are not surprising that UI and bankruptcy appear to be closer substitutes than AFDC and Medicaid with bankruptcy. Since over 30 percent of all bankruptcy filers in the PSID were unemployed at some time during the year of their filing, it makes sense that bankruptcy filers are more likely to be eligible for UI. As for AFDC and Medicaid, strict income and asset restrictions make these recipients less likely to benefit from filing.[40]   However, 9 percent of the bankruptcy filers in the PSID also received AFDC benefits in the same year they filed. Thus, AFDC and bankruptcy are substitutes, but it appears that UI is a closer substitute for bankruptcy.

VI. CONCLUSIONS

The purpose of this analysis is to determine whether individuals may receive transfer program benefits rather than file for bankruptcy. Existing research has ignored this possibility despite individuals receiving both transfer benefits and filing for bankruptcy in the same year. Both the theoretical modeling and the empirical results in the analysis presented here lend support to the hypothesis. Results using two different data sets suggest that increases in average UI and AFDC benefits decrease the number of filings. That this occurs is not surprising since all of these programs provide income- and wealth insurance.

The impending change in the bankruptcy laws makes the investigation of this topic even more relevant. Supporting evidence in Fisher (2001) suggests that increases in the bankruptcy exemptions decrease the number of UI and AFDC recipients. Thus, the proposed changes to the bankruptcy laws may unintentionally increase the number of UI and AFDC recipients.

As for the other variables used in the empirical model, the findings here match that of previous research. In the literature, the most important variable has been the bankruptcy exemptions. Hynes (1998) uses state data and finds that the exemption measures denominated in dollars have no statistically significant impact on the number of filings as well. Fay, Hurst, and White also use the PSID and find evidence that increases in the financial benefit to filing increase the probability a household files.

An important question is whether any changes by the state legislatures have contributed to the large increase in the number of bankruptcy filings. Between 1989 and 1996, the real, average state exemptions increased by approximately $876, which includes both the changes to the homestead and non-homestead exemptions.[41] At most, the $876 increase in the real bankruptcy exemptions is predicted to increase the number of filings by one thousand between 1989 and 1996. This is a relatively small effect considering the number of filings increased by more than four hundred thousand over this period.

The real value of average weekly UI benefits has also been relatively stable between 1989 and 1996; average UI benefits remained around $119. However, there has been a significant decrease in the average monthly AFDC benefits from $275 per month in 1989 to $215 per month in 1996, which could help explain the increase in the number of bankruptcy filings. From the results presented above, this 20 percent decrease in average AFDC benefits is predicted to increase the number of bankruptcy filings by approximately 50,000 over the eight years.[42] Therefore, changes in AFDC and changes in the bankruptcy laws may help explain some of the increase in the number of bankruptcy filings.

The optimal bankruptcy literature may be extended as a result of this work. Assuming the government provides a minimum level of insurance, it can provide this minimum level by altering the mix of bankruptcy exemptions, UI benefits, and AFDC benefits. For example, if the government wants to maintain a given level of insurance but wants to decrease the generosity of UI and AFDC, it could increase the bankruptcy exemptions to offset the decrease in UI and AFDC. By including transfer benefits in a model similar to Adler, Polak, and Schwartz (2000) or Wang and White (2001), a researcher could conduct this sort of experiment.

References

Adler, Barry, Ben Polak, and Alan Schwartz. 2000. "Regulating consumer bankruptcy: a theoretical inquiry. *Journal of Legal Studies* 29(2): 585-613.

Dye, Ronald A. 1986. An economic analysis of bankruptcy statutes. *Economic Inquiry* 19: 417-428.

Elias, Stephen, Albin Renauer, and Robin Leonard. 1995. *How to file for bankruptcy.* 5th ed. Berkeley, CA: Nolo Press.

Fisher, Jonathan D. 2001. Personal bankruptcy filings: the effects of government transfer programs and bankruptcy exemptions. Ph.D. dissertation, University of Kentucky.

Fay, Scott, Erik Hurst and Michelle White. 2001. The household bankruptcy decision. *American Economic Review* forthcoming.

Grogger, Jeffrey. 2001. The effects of time limits and other policy changes on welfare use, work, and income among female-headed households. *NBER working paper 8153.*

Gropp, Reint, J. Karl Scholz, and Michelle White. 1997. Personal bankruptcy and credit supply and demand. *Quarterly Journal of Economics* 112(1): 217-51.

Gruber, Jonathan. 1999. The wealth of the unemployed: adequacy and implications for unemployment insurance. *NBER working paper 7348.*

Hynes, Richard Mark. 1998. Three essays on consumer bankruptcy and exemptions. Ph.D. dissertation, University of Pennsylvania.

Meyer, Bruce D. 1990. Unemployment Insurance and unemployment spells. *Econometrica* 58(4): 757-782.

Montgomery, Edward and John C. Navin. 2000. Cross-state variation in Medicaid programs and female labor supply. *Economic Inquiry* 38(3): 402-418.

Posner, Eric A. 1995. Contract law in the welfare state: a defense of the unconscionablility doctrine, usury laws, and related limitations on the freedom to contract. *Journal of Legal Studies* 24(2): 283-319.

Stavins, Joanna. 2000. Credit card borrowing, delinquency, and personal bankruptcy. *New England Economic Review* July-Aug: 15-30.

Sullivan, Teresa, Elizabeth Warren, and Jay Westbrook. 1989. *As we forgive our debtors: bankruptcy and consumer credit in America.* New York, NY: Oxford University Press.

Wang, Hung-Jen and Michelle White. 2000. An optimal personal bankruptcy procedure and proposed reforms. J*ournal of Legal Studies* 29(1): 255-286.

White, Michelle. 1991. Economic versus sociological approaches to legal research: the case of bankruptcy. *Law & Society Review* 25(3): 685-709.

—. 1998. Why don't more households file for bankruptcy? *Journal of Law, Economics, and Organization* 14(2): 205-231.

Table 1
Comparison of bankruptcy filers and non-filers

	Non-filers (n=34,586) Mean	Filers (n=187) Mean
Whether received UI	0.112	0.155 *
Whether received AFDC	0.089	0.096
Financial benefit ($)	1,377.125	3,478.906 *
Income ($)	31,259.150	23,270.110 *
Own home	0.632	0.497 *
Head missed work	0.336	0.508 *
Tenure of head (months)	65.793	49.171 *
Age of head (years)	43.974	36.070 *
Head is male	0.748	0.722
Head is married	0.621	0.620
Divorced-widowed-separated	0.222	0.251

Notes
* Indicates the difference between the filers and non-filers is statistically significant at the 5 percent level of significance.
Data come from the Panel Study of Income Dynamics (1989-1996). The 'head is male' variable equals one if the head of the household is male. The 'own home', 'head missed work', 'head is married', and 'divorced-widowed-separated' variables equal one if the head answered yes to the question. The income variable excludes income from UI and AFDC that the household may have received in the year.

Table 2
Results using the state data

	I		II	
	Coefficient	t-statistic	Coefficient	t-statistic
Average UI benefits	-0.01032	-8.578 *	-0.01215	-9.815 *
Average AFDC benefits	-0.00212	-6.909 *	-0.00147	-3.961 *
Average Medicaid benefits	-0.00007	-2.535 *	-0.00003	-1.011
Homestead exemption	-6.84E-07	-0.780	-8.91E-07	-1.091
Non-homestead exemption	-8.05E-06	-2.372	-2.90E-06	-0.926
Garnishment allowed	0.47145	5.757 *	0.17909	2.207 *
Unlimited homestead exemption	0.12809	2.419 *	0.37612	5.381 *
Per capita personal income	-0.00004	-1.891 +	-0.00003	-1.268
Unemployment rate	0.02195	1.446	0.02447	1.743 +
% living in a MSA	0.00568	3.815 *	0.00793	5.145 *
% homeownership	0.00649	1.289	0.00639	1.257
% divorced	6.16416	3.769 *	2.97770	1.842 +
% white	0.18712	1.007	0.26376	1.355
% with health insurance	3.04823	5.826 *	1.88118	3.670 *
% aged 25-44	3.19505	2.057 *	4.16887	2.791 *
Population	-2.62E-10	-0.064	-7.54E-09	-1.632 +
Year dummy variables	YES		YES	
% employed in each sector[1]				
Mining	-4.69975	-2.171 *	3.11283	1.506
Construction	-12.16780	-5.153 *	-14.41445	-6.084 *
Manufacturing	-3.53803	-4.450 *	0.33660	0.399
Transportation and Utilities	-9.77570	-3.227 *	-4.07920	-1.343
Wholesale	9.58714	3.175 *	17.91855	6.463 *
Retail	-19.89268	-8.888 *	-14.56595	-6.433 *
Finance, Insurance and Real Estate	-5.15810	-2.750 *	-1.42097	-0.833
Service	-2.35190	-2.489 *	1.09585	1.119
Legal employment per capita	-0.32924	-6.153 *	-0.20360	-4.126 *
Banks offices per capita	-3753.194	-10.623 *	-1729.643	-4.222 *
Region fixed effects	NO		YES	
Constant	-2.72032	-3.554	-5.71386	-7.203
R-squared	0.7140		0.7157	

Notes
[1] The omitted sector is agriculture.
* Indicates the coefficient is statistically significant at the 5 percent level of significance.
+ Indicates the coefficient is statistically significant at the 10 percent level of significance.
The dependent variable equals the number of personal bankruptcy filings in the state divided by the population of the state, transformed using a logistic transformation. The data spans 1989-1996. The 'unlimited homestead exemption' variable equals one if the state allows an unlimited homestead exemption. For the region fixed effects, the nine Census regions are used.

Table 3
Results using the household data

	I		II		III	
	Marginal		Marginal		Marginal	
	impact	z-score	Impact	z-score	Impact	z-score
Average UI benefits	7.10E-06	0.63	-1.8E-05	-1.77 *	-1.6E-05	-1.77 *
Average AFDC benefits	3.73E-07	0.18	1.30E-06	0.62	1.25E-06	0.67
Average Medicaid benefits	6.34E-07	2.34	2.47E-07	0.83	2.31E-07	0.87
Financial benefit	3.02E-07	5.35 *	3.28E-07	5.39 *	2.86E-07	5.48 *
(Financial benefit)^2	-4.37E-12	-3.06 *	-4.77E-12	-3.08 *	-4.11E-12	-3.27 *
Lagged bankruptcy rate	0.6567	4.05 *	-------	-------	-------	-------
Income	-4.53E-08	-4.03 *	-4.64E-08	-3.90 *	0.0000	-3.21 *
Reduction in income	0.0002	0.58	0.0003	0.65	0.0002	0.70
Age of household head	0.0001	1.53	0.0001	1.55	0.0001	1.53
(Age)^2	-2.05E-06	-2.34 *	-2.21E-06	-2.36 *	-1.93E-06	-2.35 *
Graduated high school	-0.0001	-0.21	-9.2E-05	-0.20	-0.0001	-0.31
Graduated college	-0.0021	-4.09 *	-0.0023	-4.12 *	-0.0021	-4.04 *
Family size	0.0003	2.92 *	0.0003	2.71 *	0.0002	2.26 *
Own business	0.0008	1.56	0.0008	1.56	0.0006	1.24
Own home	-0.0001	-0.22	-0.0001	-0.29	7.79E-06	0.02
Legal employment per capita	0.0003	1.40	0.0003	1.06	0.0003	1.20
State income growth	-0.0026	-0.17	0.0032	0.22	0.0021	0.15
State income deviation	-6.04E-07	-1.05	9.06E-08	0.13	1.42E-07	0.24
Year fixed effects	YES		YES		YES	
Head missed work	-------	-------	-------	-------	0.0016	3.79 *
Tenure of head (months)	-------	-------	-------	-------	-6.56E-06	-2.40 *
Head is male	-------	-------	-------	-------	-0.0006	-0.92
Married	-------	-------	-------	-------	0.0010	1.37
Divorced-widowed-separated	-------	-------	-------	-------	0.0017	2.33 *
Pseudo R-squared	0.1317		0.1212		0.1410	

Notes
* Indicates the coefficient is statistically significant at the 5 percent level of significance.
+ Indicates the coefficient is statistically significant at the 10 percent level of significance.
The dependent variable equals one if household i filed for bankruptcy in year t. The data comes from the PSID and spans 1989-1996. All specifications use the PSID family weights. The standard errors are corrected using the "cluster" command in Stata, which recognizes the panel nature of the data. 'Reduction in income' equals one if income decreased between t and t-1. The 'own business', 'head is male', 'own home', 'head missed work', 'head is married', and 'divorced-widowed-separated' variables equal one if the head answered yes to the question. The income variable excludes income from UI and AFDC that the household may have received in the year.

Figure 1A: Number of bankruptcy filings and the Gross Domestic Product growth rate; 1972-1999

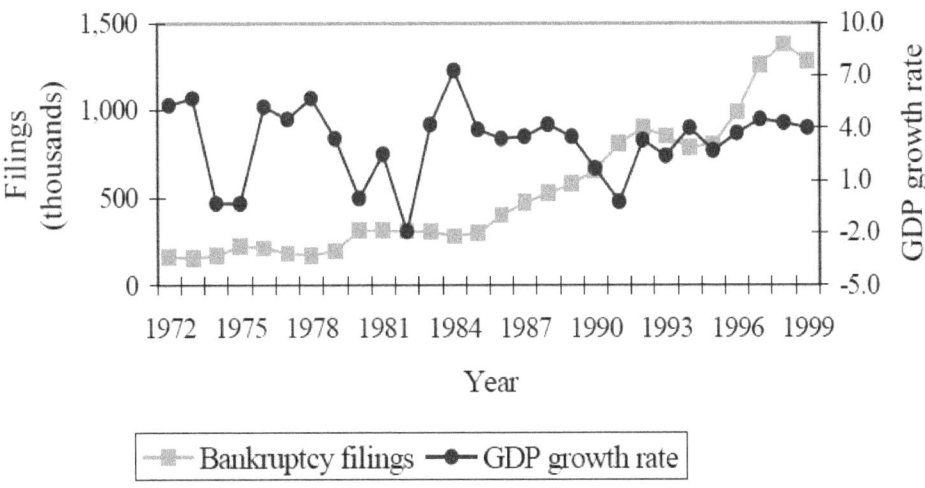

Figure 1B: Number of UI and AFDC recipients; 1972-1998

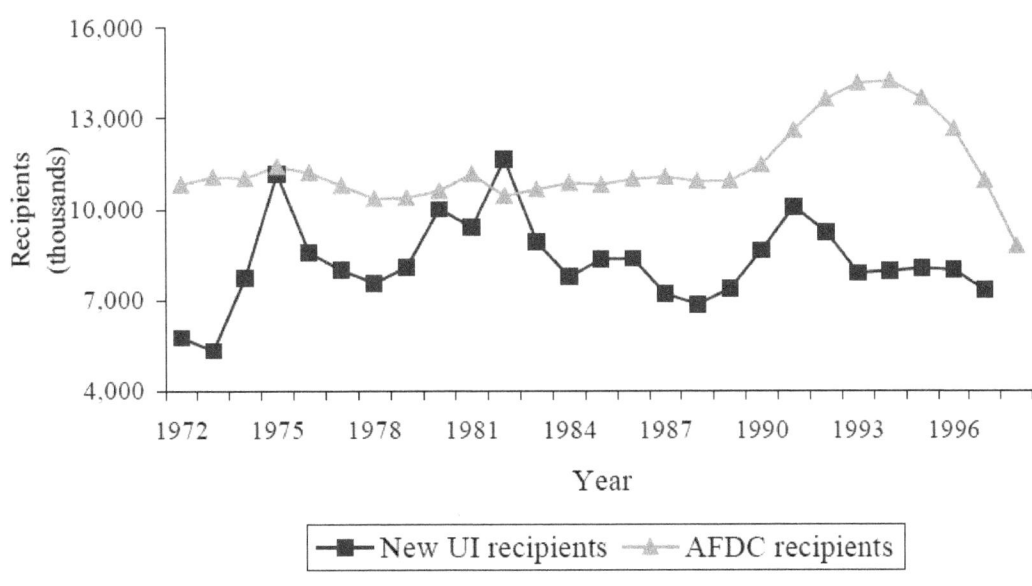

Figure 2: The bankruptcy budget constraints

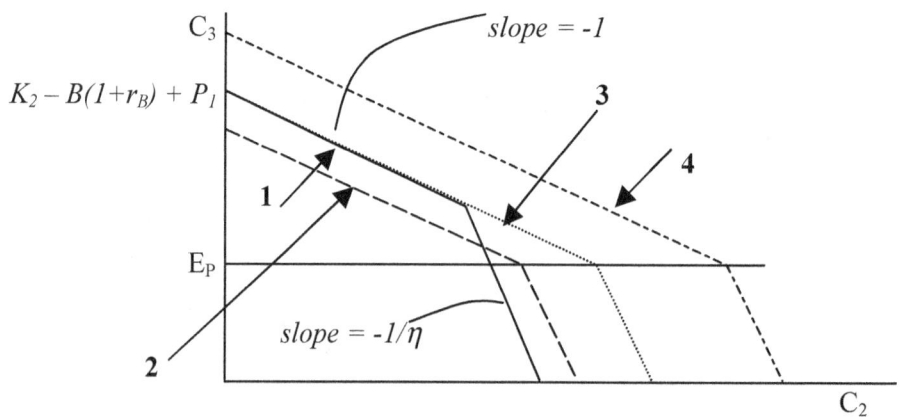

Budget constraint 1: for an individual if there is no bankruptcy program

Budget constraint 2: for an individual who benefits from filing and $(P_1 - E_P) > B(1+r_B) - R(.)$

Budget constraint 3: for an individual who benefits from filing and $(P_1 - E_P) = B(1+r_B) - R(.)$

Budget constraint 4: for an individual who benefits from filing and $(P_1 - E_P) < B(1+r_B) - R(.)$

Figure 3: Introduction of the transfer programs

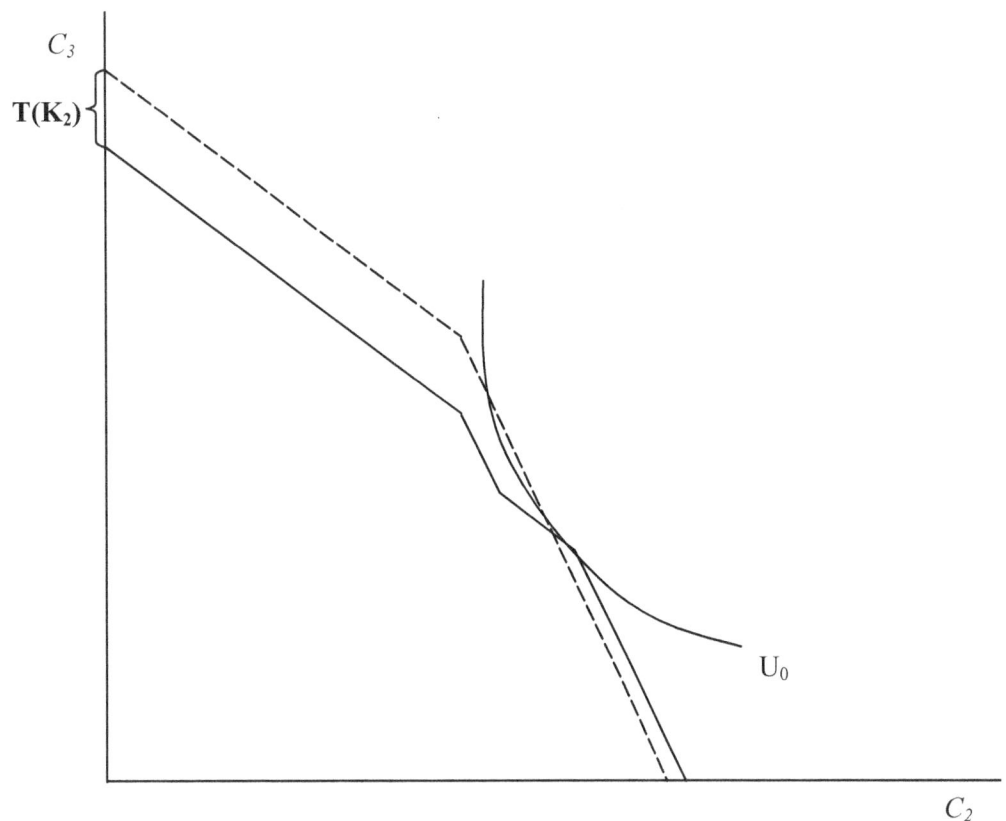

——— *Budget constraint with bankruptcy but no transfer benefits*

- - - - - *Budget constraint with the transfer benefits but no bankruptcy*

Figure 4: Comparative static result for a change in the transfer program benefit

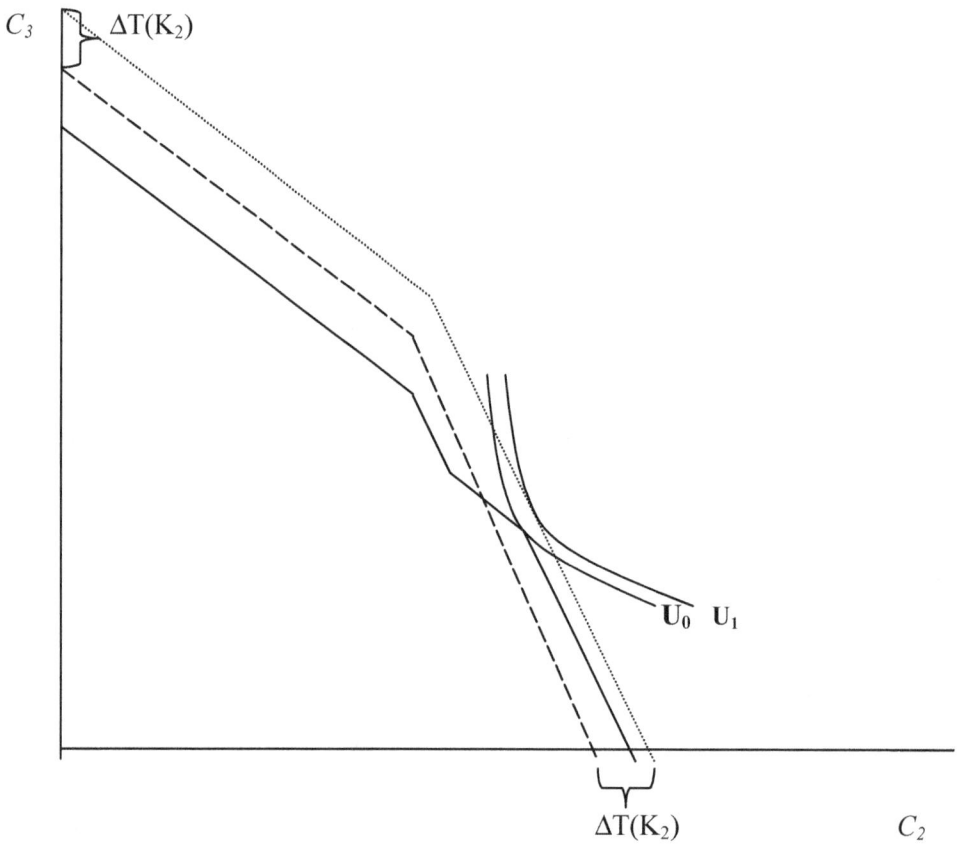

———— *Budget constraint with bankruptcy but no transfer benefits*

— — — *Budget constraint with a smaller transfer benefit but no bankruptcy*

················ *Budget constraint with a larger transfer benefit but no bankruptcy*

Appendix

For the individual to file for bankruptcy, I assume that the x-intercept increases when the individual files for bankruptcy. Intuitively, this means that if the individual consumes all of his income and assets in the second period, this amount is larger if the individual financially benefits from filing than if he does not. Mathematically:

Maximum second period consumption without bankruptcy equals

$$K_2 + \theta + \eta(P_1 - \theta) - B(1 + r_B) \qquad (A1)$$

Maximum second period consumption with bankruptcy equals

$$K_2 + \eta E_P - R(P_1, K_2, E_P, B) \qquad (A2)$$

The individual financially benefits from filing if *(A1) < (A2)*. This simplifies to:

$$(\theta - \eta) + \eta(P_1 - E_P) < B(1 + r_B) - R(.). \qquad (A3)$$

If equation (A3) holds, then the individual financially benefits from filing.

Now, comparing consumption in the third period when the individual files for bankruptcy and when he does not yields the following.

Maximum third period consumption without bankruptcy equals

$$K_2 - B(1 + r_B) + P_1 \qquad (A4)$$

Maximum third period consumption with bankruptcy equals

$$K_2 - R(.) + E_P \qquad (A5)$$

Comparing the magnitude of these terms yields the following condition:

$$(P_1 - E_P) \overset{?}{<=>} B(1 + r_B) - R(.) \qquad (A6)$$

While this is similar to the inequality in equation (A3), the sign of equation (A6) cannot be signed without at least one more assumption. Thus, an individual can benefit financially from filing and still have a decrease in the period three intercept. Budget constraint (2) in Figure 2 illustrates this case: the x-intercept increases while the y-intercept decreases.

[1] See Fisher (2001) for a review of the bankruptcy literature. Up until the late 1990s, very few personal bankruptcy papers were published. Recently, Michelle White and co-authors have published in this area. For example, see Fay, Hurst, and White (2001), Gropp, Scholz, and White (1997), and White (1991, 1998). However, the amount of research before this was not large (see footnote three).

[2] In 1997, the Federal government changed the AFDC program and renamed it Temporary Assistance to Needy Families (TANF). Since the data used in this paper ends in 1996, only data from AFDC is used. Therefore, I refer to the program as AFDC rather than TANF throughout the analysis.

[3] The amount of research by economists on UI and AFDC is not comparable to that of personal bankruptcy. Using a "words anywhere" search on EconLit, I found 1,798 hits for Unemployment Insurance, 193 hits for Aid to Families with Dependent Children (AFDC), and fifteen hits for personal bankruptcy. In addition, a search of Temporary Assistance to Needy Families (TANF), the successor to the AFDC program, yields five hits although the program has only been in existence since 1997.

[4] Meyer (1990) estimates that a 10-percentage point increase in the UI replacement rate increases the spell of unemployment by 1.5 weeks. Montgomery and Navin (2000) estimate that a 10 percent increase in AFDC benefits decreases labor supply participation by 1 percent.

[5] See Gropp, Scholz, and White (1997) for estimates of these effects.

[6] Posner (1995) put forward a similar hypothesis, stating that personal bankruptcy and transfer programs are all part of the same social safety net and that bankruptcy is "social insurance for the nonpoor".

[7] The filers received benefits from at least one of the following: Unemployment Insurance, Aid to Families with Dependent Children, Supplemental Security Income, and Food Stamps.

[8] The Bankruptcy Reform Act of 2001 would set a maximum amount of home equity ($125,000) that the filer could keep, which would override any higher state limits. In addition, if a debtor's income is sufficient to pay at least 25 percent of his debts, the filer must file under Chapter 13 rather than Chapter 7.

[9] See Fisher (2001) for a more detailed description of the personal bankruptcy laws.

[10] Unsecured debts have no collateral attached to the debt. For example, credit card debt is unsecured. A secured debt has collateral attached to it, such as a home mortgage or an automobile loan.

[11] If the filer is behind in the mortgage and is not able to maintain regular payments, the mortgage lender may foreclose on the home after the bankruptcy proceeding.

[12] Legally, there are ways to avoid turning over your home if you file. For example, the individual and the mortgage lender could come to an agreement on a payment plan that would allow to the individual to keep the home. Alternatively, if the filer has $17,000 in equity, he can pay the trustee the difference between the equity and the exemption, $2,000, to keep the home.

[13] See Wang and White (2000).

[14] Using income shocks rather than wealth shocks makes little difference in the theoretical modeling. However, the difference is significant for two reasons. First, a negative income shock may make the

individual eligible to receive transfer benefits. Second, the income shocks imply that household income should matter in the empirical specification, while Fay Hurst, and White argue that household income is not relevant in the bankruptcy decision. This difference can be tested in the empirical models.

[15] Here, I assume the individual makes the decision to file for bankruptcy given his first period choices.

[16] This could represent money in a checking account or some other liquid asset.

[17] If the individual files, the individual can also sell the remaining assets, E_P. Thus in bankruptcy, the individual can increase period two consumption by ηE_P, assuming all liquid assets are not exempt.

[18] The three bankruptcy budget constraints shown assume that the benefit to filing is positive. Since an individual only files with a positive benefit in the second period, I have not shown a budget constraint with a negative benefit. If the benefit were negative in the second period, both the x- and y-intercepts for this new budget constraint would be less than the intercepts for budget constraint (1) in Figure 2.

[19] Indirectly, Figure 2 also shows the importance of the transactions costs. If there were no transaction costs, then the budget constraint would be a straight line connecting the two, equal intercepts. Thus, if the individual benefits from filing, both the x- and y-intercepts always increase; there would be a positive income effect shifting the budget constraint parallel. In this type of model, every individual with a positive benefit would file. White (1998) estimates that at least 15 percent of all U.S. households would benefit financially from filing while only 1 percent of households actually files for bankruptcy each year.

[20] Even when the individual has the option to file for bankruptcy and receive the transfer benefits, the introduction of the transfer benefits decreases the probability the individual files for bankruptcy.

[21] Both Fay, Hurst, and White and Dye (1986) use this measure. See Fay, Hurst, and White for a more detailed description of the measurement of the benefit variable using the PSID.

[22] The exemption data were found in Elias, Renauer, and Leonard (1995).

[23] I exclude UI and AFDC income from this variable since these are my measures of transfer benefits.

[24] While the state governments and the Federal government jointly fund these programs, the states have discretion over the benefit structure and eligibility criteria for these programs.

[25] The decision to receive the transfer benefits may be correlated with the decision to file and thus correlated with the error term. This means that the actual transfer benefits received would be correlated with the error term, but the state average transfer benefits would not be correlated with the error term.

[26] Interestingly, just looking at the average UI and AFDC payments and the state filing rate, some support is generated for the basic hypothesis that states with higher transfer payments have lower filing rates. The two states with the largest UI and AFDC payments - Alaska and Hawaii, respectively - have some of the lowest filing rates (0.1 percent). The two states with the least generous transfer benefits – Louisiana and Mississippi - have average filing rates (a 0.3 percent filing rate and 0.4 rate, respectively).

[27] The sign and significance of the coefficients do not change when a logit is used rather than a probit.

[28] The number of bankruptcy filings for each state comes from the American Bankruptcy Institute's web site <http://abiworld.org>. The site was visited in August 2000.

[29] The marginal impact of a change in X with the logistic transformation equals $(\beta e^{X\beta}) / (1 + e^{X\beta})^2$.

[30] An observation in the PSID is a household year.

[31] A Hausman test was conducted to determine whether the fixed effect or random effect is more appropriate.

[32] The results for the transfer variables do not change when state fixed effects are used, but the unlimited coefficient becomes statistically insignificant as would be predicted. I use the nine Census regions.

[33] Throughout the empirical analysis, a one-sided test of significance is performed on the transfer program coefficients, the income coefficient, and the benefit/exemptions coefficients.

[34] Stavins (2000) also found that households with health insurance were more likely to file for bankruptcy.

[35] Since the bankruptcy questions were asked in 1996 only, any household not interviewed in 1996 was not be included in the data.

[36] Once a household filed for bankruptcy, additional observations from this household are not included. Mainly, these observations are not included because a household filing for bankruptcy has to wait six years before it can legally file for bankruptcy again if it received a discharge of its debts.

[37] I use a probit in all specifications. The "cluster" command from Stata is also used in all specifications. The command recognizes that the repeated observations of the households are not independent.

[38] To be consistent with the previous work, I include the same set of variables as Fay, Hurst, and White, except three. First, the lagged filing rate used here differs because they know what Bankruptcy Court district the household resides in while I do not. Thus, I use the lagged state filing rate while they used the specific district filing rate. Second, the county unemployment rate is not available in the early release data that I used. Thus, I do not include the variable. Finally, I exclude the state fixed effects. The state income deviation variable varies across states but not over time, as does the state fixed effects, which means the variables should be highly correlated. Therefore, I exclude the state fixed effects.

[39] In the state data, the marginal effect is even larger - an 8 percent increase in the average UI benefits decreases bankruptcy filings by 20 percent, which seems unusually large.

[40] To be eligible for AFDC, families must have less than $1,000 in property, but this does exclude home equity and the family automobiles.

[41] All of these dollar values are in 1982-84 dollars. Only thirteen states increased the real value of their exemptions during this period. Minnesota was the only state to decrease its exemptions during the period.

[42] This result may not be as strong as I would like since the AFDC benefits were statistically insignificant in the PSID specifications. In the state data, there is a negative and significant relationship that is not found in the PSID data. Thus, while the decrease in AFDC benefits may have contributed to the increase in the number of filings, it may not be as large as indicated by the number reported. The number should be taken as suggestive and an upper bound.